Claws, Cuddles, and Chaos

The Honest and Funny Guide to Training Your Cat

Ted Bear Burton

ISBN: 9798861334327

Copyright © 2023 Studiolo Alchemico- Ted Bear Burotn - All rights reserved. Patamu: 210583

www.studioloalchemico.com

This document is geared towards providing exact and reliable information in regard to the topic and issue covered.

- From a Declaration of Principles which was accepted and approved equally by a Committee of the American Bar Association and a Committee of Publishers and Associations.

In no way is it legal to reproduce, duplicate, or transmit any part of this document in either electronic means or in printed format. All rights reserved.

The information provided herein is stated to be truthful and consistent, in that any liability, in terms of inattention or otherwise, by any usage or abuse of any policies, processes, or directions contained within is the solitary and utter responsibility of the recipient reader. Under no circumstances will any legal responsibility or blame be held against the publisher for any reparation, damages, or monetary loss due to the information herein, either directly or indirectly.

Respective authors own all copyrights not held by the publisher.

The information herein is offered for informational purposes solely and is universal as so. The presentation of the information is without contract or any type of guarantee assurance.

The trademarks that are used are without any consent, and the publication of the trademark is without permission or backing by the trademark owner. All trademarks and brands within this book are for clarifying purposes only and are owned by the owners themselves, not affiliated with this document.

Table of Contents

Introduction

You opened the pages of this book, I welcome you to *"Claws, Cuddles, and Chaos: The Honest and Fun Guide to Training Your Cat."* If you have ever wondered if a cat can be trained as it is done with a dog, get ready for a lovely trip full of laughter, fun, and movements of your head, remembering some adventure with your cat. This is going to be a journey of learning and feline wisdom.

I have prepared a whimsical guide for you, and I, who I hope to take you along this adventure, will be the companion that will help you explore a universe as fascinating as sweet cats. Cats have a reputation for being independent by nature and acting enigmatically, but remember that they are creatures you can train. In this book, I will take you on an adventure of understanding, communication, and positive reinforcement so that you unlock the hidden potential that your cat has.

From the litter box, how to prepare it, the mistakes besides the solution, to the scratching, when this four-legged gentleman scratches the furniture and makes some mess with the nails. I will take you through the ins and outs of training with tips, humor, and various anecdotes. This journey transcends conventional notions of training, let's dismantle myths together, get to know quirks, and then go to a clear approach on how to own a cat.

In the first part of knowing the mysteries of the litter box, I will teach you how to prepare the box, the correct size, the different types of box, and the location, to solve a series of problems that can occur but have a simple solution. Then, I will show you how to apply *paw-sitive* reinforcement, which is for you to educate, teach tricks, and understand a little how they are, why they do what they do, and how you can educate them.

I will show you the complex world of its logic, understanding those meows, purrs, body positions, and scratching so that you will know how to turn it into art and stop capturing its abstract lines on the furniture. You will have solutions that honor the bond between humans and cats. This book is not a rigid training manual but a lighthearted exploration of the human-cat relationship. With each turn of the page, you'll gain insights into your cat's whimsical personality, discover the depths of their feline logic, and celebrate the triumphs and tribulations of training.

Whether you're an experienced cat enthusiast or a newcomer to the feline kingdom, this guide will inspire and entertain you, leaving you with a deep appreciation for the fascinating creatures that enrich our lives. So, cat lover, find your favorite spot, snuggle up with your whiskered buddy, and let's embark on this remarkable training, understanding, and laughter journey. Together, we will pave the way for a harmonious and fulfilling relationship with your cat, where paws and laughter dance in perfect harmony.

Chapter 1: The Cat Litter Box Chronicles

The cat litter, that throne where our furry sit to capture their footprint to the world, where they leave their residue every day and cover it, well, sometimes, when they are lazy, they leave that picture there to see it as a rock on the beach and if we claim... We are ignored by those scoundrels.

Choosing cat litter is not easy, or it can be if you read this chapter where I will tell you how you choose, prepare, and use it for your beautiful feline.

Choosing the Right Cat Litter

The first part of this chronicle is to find the right litter for the cats they like so that they do not leave their gift outside or in the bathroom that we like, perform, and are of quality. I detail each type with its pros and cons.

If you start in the world of cats, you will surely be surprised by the different types of litter and may have trouble finding the best litter. Many people want to know the various options that exist, and when they see the cats, they do not know what to do. I describe each of them with the pros and cons.

Clay Litter

It is one of the most popular litters you will find; You can find it on any cat supply site. Many brands fit any pocket; you can have it with or without an aroma or a binder.

Clay occurs naturally and can be easily found, making it a great choice for litter. Its disadvantage is that it generates a lot of dust, and some marks leave a film all over the room and mark on the cat's paws. This is especially true if it's a covered litter box where dust can get trapped.

Some cats can have breathing problems if they inhale a lot of concentrated clay dust. Therefore, binder litter is also preferred, as it is easier to clean and traps odors better than litter that does not clump.

Walnut Litter

It is a great option instead of clay, it has little dust. As you can see, nut litter is crushed shells, it's very absorbent and renewable, so it's great for the environment. Hygienic walnut litter is gentle on the kitten's paws and does not leave traces at home. The only downside is that it does not clump, which means that you have to stir it frequently to ensure that the nutshells can fully absorb the urine, and if the urine stays at the bottom for a long time, it can start to smell bad. Walnut litter also tends to be dark, which makes it difficult to find the nuggets left by our felines as a gift for us.

Tofu Litter

This is one of the newest alternatives in cat litter. It is a binder, so it is easy to clean and the agglomeration helps reduce odors. It is a little more expensive than others, and this is a disadvantage. It can be hard to find too, but it uses renewable materials and is a great alternative to clay if you want dust-free binder litter.

Silica gel litter

This is one of the strangest on this list, it is a very absorbent material that can quickly absorb and retain moisture with which it comes into contact, so it does a great job absorbing moisture and reducing odor despite being a non-binding litter.

The disadvantage is that it must be mixed frequently to distribute the urine and that it is better absorbed and in addition, it is very expensive.

Litters with diatomaceous ground

These litters are another non-binding that is very, very absorbent. It works quickly to engross urine, and with agitation every so often, it will absorb moisture from the feces when our cat's gift looks like a flan. It can also help you reduce odor.

The disadvantage is that the larger stone size is expensive and can make our demanding feline king dislike it.

Lawn

In this case, make litter for lawns from grass seeds, and like clay litter, you buy it as agglomerating or non-binding litter. It is biodegradable and renewable, so it will not harm the environment.

You can even flush some marks in the toilet, although it is complex to find in some places, there is no downside to using grass in the litter box.

Paper

This is very absorbent, if you like silica gel, you should stir the litter to spread the urine evenly frequently. I like recycled paper, but I realized it didn't do enough to treat odors at home to use daily.

If you have more than one cat using the same box, recycled paper can become a soggy mess.

Corn

Corn is cheaper and renewable, so it is perfect as an alternative to clay. It is quite light and creates tight lumps that can be easily pulled out. I find that tight clumping helps to use less litter, so it pays for itself over time.

Pine litter

It is unique because it has a fresh pine aroma that can hide the smells of our cat's gifts, thus keeping the house fresh. Pine trash looks like grass and you find it both binder and non-binder.

The only disadvantage is that some people cannot enjoy the smell of Christmas throughout the year.

Cat Litter Box Configuration

So you are going to prepare your cat's litter box.

The first thing to keep in mind is that you see the size of the box you will use for the cat. You cannot have it too small because tight spaces are not fun for anyone, or do you like a tight bathroom where you sit, your knees touch the wall, and your shoulder brushes the sink?

Make sure the boxes are large enough for the cat to fit inside, with some room to spare. They should have ample space for you to move and dig in the place without having to leave. There should be plenty of room to avoid any deposits you still have from previous visits.

As a rule, the litter box should be at least as long as the cat, from the nose to the tip of the tail when it is extended. And the width should be at least as wide as the cat is long, but not with the tail extended.

Location of the Cat Litter Box

In what has to do with the location of the litter box, you have to be attentive toward it. It must be:

- Easy access: The cat should have at least two ways to get to and from the litter box. This is to prevent the litter box from being completely blocked, for example, by the dog, another cat, a closet door, etc. If they can't get there or walk away with confidence, they may not use it.

- Enough space: even if you have a good number of boxes, there must be diverse litter boxes to avoid problems. It gives me something when I see a house with enough litter boxes according to the number of cats and size, although I have seen others where they line up litter boxes next to each other. It is best to put litter boxes in different spaces. If you must put them in the same room, there should be plenty of space between them.

- Let the air circulate: The cat's nose is very sensitive, and putting the litter box in a small closet or a dirty basement may cause it to deal with odors and can stress it.

Things to Avoid When Putting the Cat Litter Box

Please note:

- Draft ventilation: These heating vents, or air conditioners, can create drafts that they don't expect, which can scare and stress you out. Avoid locating boxes near these sites.

- Personal traffic: if the cat has to deal with the possibility of people walking or running, especially if there are children next to the throne of our feline, surely the cat will not do it. It is not comfortable for them to try to find a place where so many people do not pass.

- Noise: Going to the bathroom is vulnerable for cats, who get on high alert when they are here. If they do their thing and there is a lot of noise, especially loud or sudden ones, you will rob them of the peace of the moment. In laundry rooms, people commonly put boxes, but the dryer's noise, alarms, and so on can make the cat feel exposed.

Amount of Cat Litter to Use

Filling the cat's litter is mostly straightforward, but you should know some things to help you get the ideal setup for the feline.

The ideal depth of litter depends on the cat's digging preferences, its collecting habits, and the type of litter you use. If your cat doesn't dig much, you can get away with using an inch or two of litter in the box, as long as you're diligent about picking up debris several times a day and the litter stays solid and clean. However, even in those ideal conditions for case maintenance, a couple of inches may not be enough. To make sure, I recommend starting with two to three inches of litter in each box and then adjusting as needed and replenishing to maintain that depth.

You can consider using a litter attractant, especially if your cat has learned to use litter boxes. Adding a little attractant to the litter can be caring in helping your cat become attracted to the litter and use it to do its business.

It's good to have your vet check your cats to ensure there's no medical issue keeping them away from the litter box in case you've experienced any problems in that regard.

Cat Litter Box Maintenance

The importance of collecting the stools left by the cat, wet and citrus balls and long buns at least once daily cannot be overstated.

Many studies show that cats routinely and purposefully prefer clean boxes over ones that already have accumulated waste. After all, would you rather clean a newly used toilet or one that's fuller?

In case you have money and are considering buying one of those expensive litter boxes that clean themselves, it is important to note that there are many complaints that cats get scared by the noise they make and the movement they generate. Therefore, I do not advise you to use them.

In addition, it is important to observe the trends your cat shows about the litter box. Self-cleaning boxes can deprive cats of this experience; some may reject or avoid them. In my opinion, they are an unnecessary expense and are not always well received by felines.

Wash, Rinse, Repeat

To avoid accumulating embedded litter, cat gifts besides bacteria, try to wash the litter box completely and refill it once a month. Use soap and water to wash them, but don't bleach or harsh cleaners. The smell of bleach can cause the cat not to go to the box.

To finish, dry the boxes and add clean litter. Depending on how many cats you have and how dirty they are, you may need to make complete changes between monthly box washes or wash them more frequently.

Stay tuned

Changes in the cat's urine or defecation can be clear signs of problems such as diseases or medical conditions. That's why it's important to monitor the amount and size of urine lumps and fecal deposits in the boxes each day when you take them out.

Get a large litter box, as I said before, choose the size well, but the bigger the better, it all depends on the size you have, find one with a hood to prevent the litter from coming out and to guide the cat, but remove the door, these trap bad odors, and it is good for you, but cats do not, they will feel like they enter a portable toilet on a construction site, a Friday after all the workers have used it.

Troubleshoot Cat Litter Box Problems

The cat can often avoid using the litter box due to behavioral problems, discomfort, or stress. Medical reasons can also affect its use, so it is important to pay attention to changes in its behavior and take the cat to the vet for a review if problems are observed.

Metabolism problems, such as diabetes and kidney disease, can increase the amount of urine the cat produces, making it difficult to get to the litter box on time.

If the cat is arthritic, it may have difficulty climbing stairs or entering a litter box with high walls, which may lead it to avoid its use.

Painful urination, which can occur due to lower urinary tract disorders, can also prevent the cat from using the litter box properly.

Elimination-related pains, such as constipation or diarrhea, can be unpleasant for the cat and cause it to avoid the litter box.

In addition, if the cat has pain in the paws that makes it difficult to walk on the litter, it can also be a reason to avoid the box.

In the case of older cats, dementia can cause them to forget where the litter box is or how to use it properly if they find it. Older cats can sometimes forget training due to problems with cognitive dysfunction, similar to Alzheimer's in cats.

It's critical to be on the lookout for any changes in your cat's behavior and take them to the vet if you notice they're having difficulty using the litter box to rule out medical issues and ensure their well-being.

Next Steps

After you confirm that nothing happens with the cat, the next thing is you address the reasons why it does not use the litter box as it should, for example:

- I had a cat with separation anxiety that wouldn't stop meowing and almost screaming when alone, so the cat put down the box and took two weeks to adjust to it again.

- On another occasion, I found a cat, and I sobbed it on the street, then when I returned home, my cat was upset and smelled me for a while, which caused me to leave the litter box for a couple of days.

- Believe it or not, cats also get stressed, on one occasion, a friend told me that at home, they began to raise a building and the cat was stressed with so much noise and fuss and moved away from the litter box, outside, on the carpets, and even in bed.

- A bored or sedentary cat may have problems with the box, so give them plenty of toys and daily playtime so they exercise and don't get so bored.

Smelly litter box

Cats like clean toilets and tend to look for other spaces to vacate the tank when they are with that box full. If this happens, you have to clean it, remember that cats have a good sense of smell and a smell that you notice slightly, for them, it is intense, 14 times more, according to studies. Then it changes frequently.

When you locate it wrong

If your cat does not have privacy, the cat may not do its things, a companion had the litter on its balcony, and the cat did not like to be seen semi-sitting doing its things, the cat had to place the litter in a room away from prying eyes.

Wrong size litter box

Small cats do not care about the size of the litter box, but if you already have a cat lord, they may need a bath according to the measure I told you before, even bigger, like twice their size. Large cats can hang from the edge of the litter box and leave the gift scattered between the edge and the floor and go... You'll have to clean more.

There are the big ones who, when located, turn the box over, and all the litter falls on their backs. Surely you have seen videos like this on the internet. Years ago, it happened to me like this, the cat watered it in the middle of the night, and the next day I woke up, there was litter and debris all over the house, even on a piece of furniture. Good start to the day I got.

Not enough litter boxes

When you have several kittens at home, it is important to pay attention to their behavior regarding the litter box. If you notice irritability or tension between them around the litter box, it is advisable to provide an individual litter box for each cat.

Although small cats usually share the litter box, larger cats may fight to control this property. A cat may take possession of the box and try to prevent others from using it, which can lead to conflicts and fights between them.

It is important to note that cats have a territorial sense and may see the litter box as part of their territory. Therefore, providing individual litter boxes gives cats their personal space, and competition is avoided.

If you have several cats at home, try to place litter boxes in different rooms or on separate floors so that a specific cat does not guard them. This will help avoid confrontations and tensions between them.

Even unique cats may require more than one litter box, as some prefer to have one for their liquid needs and another for their solid needs. Providing multiple litter boxes can also help keep them cleaner and prevent them from becoming saturated quickly.

Substrate problem

To ensure litter box loyalty, keep an eye out for the type of litter your cat likes, and once you find that mark, don't change it. Cats love their comfort zone, and any change can provoke a negative reaction from the feline.

The best cat litter absorbs moisture, contains debris and odors effectively, and is great for cat well-being. If you prefer a particular product, you can start to get your cat used to that litter when it's young. However, once cats are adults, they can be more resistant to changes, although if you've tested and eliminated the causes of litter box problems, changing litter may be a good idea.

Chapter 2: Paw-sitive Reinforcement

Surely you have some toys for your cat to play with at home, or when you go to the supermarket, grab the food or litter, you find that treat you know they like and throw it in the cart.

In this chapter, I will talk about sweets, toys, and the importance of attention for them, how to take advantage of this to beat those stubborn and train them, and see what you can.

The Power of Goodies

At any given time, if you check my bag, you'll find a lot of varied goodies. These I use to teach tricks to the cat and are different from the ones I use when I cut their nails. The reward I use at home differs from the one I use outside.

How do you know what reward can be used for each situation? Start by understanding that there are high- and low-value treats, and use them strategically.

Each cat will have its taste for the treats. Generally speaking, their preferences will depend on their daily diet. Feeding them a processed food diet will make it difficult to compete with those treats, such as feeding a child potato chips and then offering granola as a treat; they will want more French fries.

It's not about finding the best treats but feeding them a healthy and nutritious diet. If you want the cat to accept a variety of rewards, you should start by feeding them healthy, moisture-rich foods. Dry food is not suitable as the main food for the cat, as they need moisture in their diet.

It is important to understand that dry food companies seek to monopolize the cat's taste buds. They formulate dry food so that cats become addicted to kibble and become loyal customers for life.

If cats are constantly fed dry food and have access to it all day, it will reduce their motivation to receive other rewards during training.

To develop the cat's food motivation, it is necessary to change the approach and offer small scheduled meals three times a day. If the cats are absent for many hours, they can use automatic feeders to ensure that you eat a healthy, moisture-rich diet. By doing this, you will see improvements in the cat's motivation for food and it will be easier to find effective rewards for training.

My favorite treats

When choosing treats for my cat, I take into account:

- Treats must be healthy, I move away from those that are processed and limit myself to something that has one or several natural ingredients.

- Small treats and gifts help the cat motivate itself while preventing weight gain. If the cat spends a lot of time chewing, it slows down the workout.

- Dry treats are easier for me to train, although sometimes training with wet ones also serves me. Working with dry food is simpler; you can pull treats to increase activity.

Before we get into the mistakes that are made when trying to train your cat, I leave you tips that you have to apply for the correct use of tricks or behavior problems.

- Use the right size, workout treats have to be small bites, not only because the mouth is small but because it can damage the appetite in a short time.

- Use the cat's food, if it tends to make fun of what you give it, it turns the learning experience. Feed the cat with small bites during training.

- They only serve the top quality treats and offer good treats when you try to train to be interested.

- Don't leave food out, you're more likely to give up for a treat if you know what you have isn't waiting for you.

Use of treats for training

Cats may not show the same outward signs of attention as a dog but don't worry, they can pay attention to you, and you can train them.

Use treats to lure them out of whatever space they are in and reward just the fact that they came to explore. Start rewarding the cat for doing a behavior like coming when you call it by name. Don't follow it or allow it to change your location.

While the cat does the behavior consistently, try training it in different spaces and circumstances. Try changing the keyword you call it, such as "Cat, come," instead of just using the treat. It's a step that may require a little patience, and it's a good idea to offer the treat periodically when you want the behavior to continue.

Try to get them to do the behavior more than once in a row. Cats may require more patience when you train them, but the important thing is that you remember to have consistency. Although the cat may not have anxiety about pleasing, it is good that you do.

Common misunderstandings

Cat owners have training problems, and they come from a misunderstanding of the cat. While this one may love you as a human companion, the personalities are different from that of dogs.

Your cat has no attention span

Cats have a large attention span; they can wait for a long time for the prey or see potential prey from their window. My cats spend their life watching the birds fly from the balcony and dream of catching a poor deluded one day!

The perceived loss of attention when you train has more to do with manipulation. Cats know that if attention is diverted, you will likely chase them, not vice versa. When this happens, make it clear that the food and reward will go away if you don't pay attention so that you can see an increase in concentration.

Looks boring

This may be a sign that I don't understand what you're trying to achieve. Consider alternatives to alleviate negative behaviors. Move the litter box to another site, try different materials for the scraper, and change the site plants. It's just adjusting the training.

Boredom can be a sign that it is not hungry for the treat, try to do it later so that you do not peck and get hungry. The cat may develop an interest if it has more appetite.

Training the cat

Treats can be very helpful for them to reinforce when training. Make sure you choose the best ones they like and are of quality. You can even use the same food from them after they go a while without eating.

Training the cat requires patience and perseverance. The cat may not seem very eager to learn new tricks like the dog, but over time you can train them to do a series of actions that may seem impossible at first.

Use this space to create a bond with the cat and enrich the natural curiosity; with a good treat, you can be closer.

The trick of sitting pretty

Here are the steps to teach it:

- You sit on the floor next to the cat; if not, you can put the cat on a table or raised surface.

- When the cat sees you have a treat, it may walk up to you and say, "Sit down," and you bring the treat over its head.

- It may stop and sit down. When the back touches the floor, you click and then give it the treat. The click can be done with a clicker or a pen with a button up to press it.

Sitting training can be tedious for cats to come in when called, so keep the sessions brief. When the cat sits constantly, it's a good sign. There you can fade the click and reward it for a well-done job.

When the cat learns to sit, it's just a matter of lifting the treat something enough on its head so that it sits on its paws and reaches for it. When the cat does, you give the cat positive reinforcement, fill it with love, and give the treat.

High Five

That it high-fives seems impressive, but the truth is an easy trick, just like teaching what it feels like, make sure that the cat and you are at the same visual level. Hold the treat in front of it at shoulder level, and when the cat reaches out its paw and touches its hand with the treat, you click and give it the treat.

The cat will soon understand that you must touch the hand before receiving the treat, at that moment, you stop holding the treat, and when it touches you, you click. When the cat agrees, start offering its hand with its palm up high-fives and give it the verbal signal you want.

When the cat touches the palm, you click and give it the treat.

Coming when called

- Wait for your cat to approach you.
- When the cat does, click with the clicker and reward it with a treat.

- Repeat this process and use a keyword, such as "come" or your name, to associate the behavior with the command.

Paw up

- Show a treat in your closed hand.

- Your cat will probably try to reach it with the paw.

- When your cat touches your hand with the paw, click and then give it the treat.

- Repeat until your cat raises its paw without hesitation when sees your closed hand.

Rotate in circles

- Hold a treat near your cat's nose and move it in a gentle circle.

- The cat should follow the treat and turn in circles.

- When your cat completes the spin, click and give it the treat.

- Repeat until your cat turns without needing to guide it with the treat.

Jump on an object

- Place an object your cat can jump under, such as a stick or hoop.

- Hold a treat on the other side of the object so it has to jump to reach it. When your cat jumps, click and give it the treat.

- Repeat this process until the cat jumps without hesitation when the cat sees the treat.

Roll

- Place your cat on its side on a comfortable surface.

- Show a treat in front of its nose and gently move it to the side.

- As you follow the treat, it should roll on its back.

- Click with the clicker and give the treat when the cat completes the roll.

Sit and sit still

- Wait for your cat to feel natural.

- While sitting, wait a few seconds before clicking the clicker.

- Then, give your cat the treat as a reward.

- Gradually increase the time it must sit before receiving the reward.

Jump to a designated surface

- Place a pillow or platform near a chair or other raised surface.

- Show a treat there and encourage it to jump.

- Click with the clicker and give the treat when the cat does.

- Repeat this process several times to make your cat comfortable jumping to the designated surface.

Turn off the light

- Place a string or chain around the light switch.

- Move it gently so that it touches the string and turns off the light.

- Click with the clicker and give the treat as a reward when the cat does.

Search and bring

- Use a small toy that your cat likes.

- Throw it a short distance away and wait for me to bring it back.

- Click with the clicker and give the treat when the cat does

- Add commands like *"search"* and *"bring"* to associate behavior with commands.

Sitting on the back

- Sit on the floor with your legs straight.

- Show a treat on your back.

- Encourage your cat to jump up and sit on your back.

- Click with the clicker and give the treat when the cat does it correctly.

Nose pointing

- Hold a small, sturdy object in front of your cat at nose level.

- Wait for the cat to touch the object with the nose.

- Click with the clicker and give the treat as a reward when the cat does.

- Use this technique to guide it in different positions or directions.

Toy Hour

Each cat has its personality and way of acting, it may have different preferences for play, or it may do them all, so they are.

In the different types of games that can make the cat participate, we have:

- Lying on the side, the cat bites and grabs a toy with the front paws and kicks sharply with the hind legs.

- Lying close to the ground, jump forward on a moving toy on the floor.

- The cat jumps and stretches in the air to grab some aerial toys.

When buying a toy, look for features that allow the cat to carry a preferred play style. Some of the most valuable tips to choose for the cat include:

- Consider the type of toy.

- Toys that are fishing rod type allow you to interact with the cat with quick and straight movements on the ground, which imitate the movements of the prey that a cat would hunt. It's a style of toy that's pretty good for kids because it gives them a hands-off approach to playing with the cat.

- There are automatic play toys for cats to play with without you having to participate, ranging from simple balls to electronic toys. Do not forget to always finish with a sweet or food so that this hunt is a reward.

- Think about the size of the toy, cats usually prefer smaller toys because they look more like normal prey, such as a bird or mouse.

- Larger stuffed toys can also be good if the cat likes to grab and bite the toy and rake it with its hind legs.

- Buy toys made of faux fur or feathers because textures have been found to encourage play because they feel more like prey. Wrinkled materials can also stimulate the cat's senses. Avoid any parts that can be detached and eaten, such as bells or plastic noses and eyes.

- You may or may not use catnip. Some toys bring this and also other similar plants, such as valerian, that can encourage the cat to investigate a toy and participate in a game. Don't worry if the cat seems to have other interests. It has been found in research that between 5% and 70% of cats respond to catnip.

A Fun Cat Game You Can Do

Now start playing with your cat friend, start with a basket of toys ready, and spend about 15 minutes each day a couple of times. This will give the cat exercise and mental stimulation. Doing so does not bore them and will prevent them from gaining weight.

Try a cat toy with a string on a stick, you can also use a laser pointer or a light toy, with the cane toy or the toy that has snap closure, you can let the cat see, plan, chase, and catch. Try to make sure that it ends with the pleasure of a good catch.

One tip is that you can rotate the stash of toys to make the matter feel interesting.

Prepare a DIY toy to keep them busy

Try to play with the cat with one or more toys for home that are excellent, and you can make or arrange them yourself.

- One option is ping pong balls or balls of this type that you have at home
- Corks
- Pompoms
- Spring-wrapped pipe cleaners
- Paper towel or roll of toilet paper
- Ice cubes

- A ball of aluminum foil

Play together without toys

If you don't have a toy handy or want to do something else, you can play with the cat using your own hands. For example, extend your finger and encourage the cat to follow you, move it behind your head or out of sight, and encourage it to hunt you.

You can also put your hands or feet under a blanket or rug and move them for the cat to investigate.

However, it is important to note that some playful and active cats may use claws as part of play. Therefore, it is advisable to teach the cat to be kind and to retract the claws. If you feel nervous about bites or scratches, you can wear a glove to protect your hand during the game.

Play hide & seek, tag, or search with the cat

Those games you played with your friends when you were a child are also fun for you to play with your cat, you can try the classics, marking, hiding, and looking for the cat to be curious and get involved and link it with them.

- Hide & seek: this is something that both can play, you call and look for the cat, and you will be happy when you find it or hide and let the cat find you. Remember, cats love to hide, so looking for them every day can be fun for both of you. If you're going to hide and hope the cat finds you, make sure the cat plays with you. Pull a wind-up toy to chase it, then hide and see if they find you.

- Tag: make the cat chase you and let it catch you, when it runs away, you can follow it and label it with a boo and a rub.

- Bring: As dogs, some cats run after objects when you throw them. Some pounce and throw the object, and others will return it, even a cat may pick up what you throw with its mouth and return it to you or put it near you. Try looking for elastic items that blow farther away or use simple things from home like made paper, a ball or a bow of hair.

Spend time brushing

Many cats like to be brushed and spend time near them, brushing them removes dirt and dead hair and improves the cat's skin when you remove skin scales and improve circulation.

Watch Cat TV

You can put an aquarium or a bird channel on TV or mobile, you can even put a bird feeder outside the house for the cat from inside to see. You can watch a kitten show together.

Make a cat treat puzzle

Try to place cat treats inside a closed box and cut holes that are large enough to put the paws, this will encourage the cat to get inside and make plans to get the treats. You can also turn a roll of toilet paper into a cat treat dispenser, fold it at the ends, and make a hole in or in the middle. The cat will learn to hit the stand until the treats come out.

Praise the cat when you discover it.

Have a playground

This is a fact, cats love cardboard boxes and paper bags that do not have handles. Put some at home for them to investigate. Flip some sides and leave others with the right side up for a change. Try putting some treats or toys inside to encourage exploration and hunting. There are boxes in different elevations, and they are fun too.

I leave you a tip from my own experience if you work from home with the cat, try to place a box the size of your cat on the desk so that the cat can curl up nearby and be part of your workday. Surely the box will be more interesting than the keyboard, although I do not promise you anything, remember, each cat is different.

Set up cat apps on your tablet

You may not believe this, but there are cat phone apps that are made for them to do things. They simulate a hiding place or look for the instincts of prey, which they love. Search the app store for cat apps, and you will see the variety they have.

Blow bubbles

Apply the typical commercial bubble wand or make one yourself with diluted dish soap, and you can make a series of bubbles nearby, you will see how it runs to catch them. The cat will enjoy watching you make bubbles and may try to catch the ones that fall or are in the air. It is an activity that can be fun for them to spend some time together in the yard or the sloping mid-afternoon sun that they like the most.

Take a nap

Cats sleep about 16 hours daily, often ready to nap. If you've been sitting still or in an activity for a while, they may approach, meow, or get your attention.

It's the perfect time for you to play with them or go to the couch to have them curl up soon. Cats love to cuddle with their parents, make cookies on you, and hit each other with your chin. It is an activity that they can do and is also part of the connection they seek to have.

Affection and Attention

There are cats that, by nature, are more affectionate than others, Siamese or Persians are known to curl up in the lap, and the Tonquinese will not only curl up, but they will tell you things in their cat language.

But, if your cat seems to prefer to be on their own at any given time, there are ways they can make relationships that last a lifetime.

Start socializing when your cat is young

The moment you bring the handsome cat home for the first time, let them get used to the new sights, smells, and sounds of the house and the whole environment. Allow them to be in a room of the house with the necessary resources for the first few days, and then introduce them to the rest of the house and some other pets.

Gradually, allow you and other household members to pet and touch the cat without forcing it. If you introduce your cat to children, make sure they are aware that they should not grab it, as this can affect the relationship and scare the charming little animal.

Confirm that they have everything their little hearts want from day one

Leave the water bowl and food accessible but away from other pets. Remember that you need one of each resource for each pet and an additional one. The same goes for litter, as I said in their respective chapter.

The scratching posts and high hangers they can access have what it takes to make you feel safe and control everything. This may relax you and bring out the social side.

Learn to speak cat language

Later I will dedicate a space to talk about this in more detail, I anticipate that you must know the language of your cat, the position of the tail, eyes, and ears say a lot, and you must know when the cat is happy or when it shows signs of stress and anxiety.

When you are in front of your cat, you can blink slowly and with this, you tell that you love it, even if you do not stare at it, because they will take the cat as a threat and the cat can run away. Half-closed eyes, forward-facing ears, and relaxed whiskers are a sign that they are relaxed and content.

Don't force it

Let the cat take the first step, don't grab it or force it to sit on you, let it come to you on its terms, that's how they are. You can also let them go free when they start to look uncomfortable or want to escape. This will help boost their confidence and make them more eager to come back to you another time.

Sometimes the cat becomes a purring machine, and usually, they like to be touched and stroked near the base of the ears, down the cheeks, and under the chin, where the facial glands are located. They don't want you to stroke them on the belly, tail, or back. Although sometimes they can be relaxed and lie down with their stomach facing the sky, it is not an invitation for you to caress them, and they could bite you. If they look at you and blink slowly, they want to be petted.

Set aside some time for them

Many cats have an active moment when dawn and dusk, it may seem like crazy running around the house and jumping, just when you sleep or want to relax, it seems like a madman who makes noise and knocks things down.

This is an instinct that they have, and it comes from nature which is when they would have hunted. Avoid trying to play with your cat at this time. The best space for them to play is when you see it wanting to do so, there you invest about 15 minutes of play.

Be approachable!

You sit with a cushion or a blanket that the cat likes and wait for it to approach you, as they will have left the smell on the blanket, they will have associations with it and may feel positive when coming. You can tempt them with a small gift to come closer, and then they smell you and will feel happier to explore more. Don't move early or scare them because this will put them off, but take the time and create a relaxed atmosphere.

Help them groom themselves

Cats are very clean beings and spend time grooming, when they develop a close bond with the cat, and it is happy to be with you, try grooming it for a while, this will not only strengthen the bond but, as I said before, brushing prevents dead hair from staying, tangled and spreading natural oils on the skin and coat and be more careful and beautiful.

Have a bond with the cat

The recipe for a real friendship with the cat is easier than you think, give them space when they need it, pamper them, and make sure they have what they need. You can give them treat and playtime, and you'll see how soon they come to you. In other words, they will wrap you around their little paw in no time.

To create an atmosphere of relaxation and tranquility, you can help the cat feel more sociable, consider plugging in a feline diffuser where the cat spends more time and thus give the cat constant comfort.

Chapter 3: Feline Logic and Compromise

You love cats, I understand it, I love them too, I adore them, they are part of my life. But sometimes it's hard to understand them, it's like trying to fit in with the love of our life, we have complex and simple things, and we have to put everything together.

In this chapter, I will help you understand behavior and get them to connect and share spaces and tips to make a living together even more pleasant.

Understanding Cat Behavior

The creator of the Garfield cartoon, Jim Davis, once said that everyone deep down is motivated by the same impulses and that cats dare to live by them. This explains why cats act the way they do and why they are considered independent.

Perhaps cats are trying to teach us a valuable lesson by acting the way they were born to act. However, this does not mean they cannot learn to behave in ways that help the family. There is hope if a cat shows excessive grooming habits, scratches or kneads destructively, or bothers a lot during the night.

Intervening early with behavioral training, veterinary supervision, or a feline behavior specialist can help fix cat behavior problems.

Normal cat behavior

Cats and people have personalities and characteristics that make them unique, so there is no definitive list of normal behavior in them. Although there are many common behaviors, keep in mind that each cat is unique and can act in different ways according to its personality and how it feels. An example is that cats can purr, groom, knead and climb, but each one does it differently. Pay attention to how the cats do and determine what's normal for the feline so you're aware of unusual behavior that may require you to take them to the doctor.

Purrs

Many people consider purring a universal sign that the cat is happy and content, as they tend to purr when they are comfortable and happy. They do this when you pet them, enjoy the sun, or sit at your computer while you work. However, purring can also be a sign of stress, especially in situations or environments unfamiliar to them. It can also occur when the cat has injuries or illnesses.

When a cat purrs, the vibrating cords of the larynx create vibrations in their body that can help them relax in the face of stress. However, if the cat purrs a lot or in situations where it normally does not, it may be a sign of illness or injury. It is important to check the cat in detail or take it to the veterinarian, especially if we notice changes in its behavior, such as lack of appetite, dehydration, or drastic changes in its usual behavior.

Toilet

Cats can spend a long time grooming, some may even spend half of their time doing this activity. In addition to keeping their fur clean, spit helps insulate their bodies and keep them warm. Therefore, you may see them grooming more frequently when it's cold.

Each cat has its own way of grooming and creating grooming patterns. It is important to pay attention to how they are cleaned because if they do it in excess or if we notice hair loss, it is advisable to take them to the veterinarian to check them and rule out any health problems.

Damage from kneading

Another common behavior of cats is kneading. It consists of pushing the front legs in and out in a movement similar to that used to knead bread, but in this case, they do it on surfaces such as pillows, pant fabrics, or even digging the nails into what they have underneath.

Although it is not certain why cats knead, some theories suggest that it may be a residual effect of breastfeeding when they were kittens or simply a way to show satisfaction. Other experts point out that cats have glands in their paws, and they could be marking the territory when kneading.

If kneading causes damage or discomfort, it's important to make sure the cat's nails are trimmed. If the cat kneads and hurts, you can distract it by petting it, playing with its paws, or giving it a treat. It is not advisable to scold or punish the cat for this behavior, as they do it instinctively and would not understand the reason for the reprimand. Let us always remember to be understanding and careful with our feline friends.

Climbing in everything

Cats love to climb everywhere, and this is due to their genetic behavior as natural predators. Climbing gives them a broader perspective of their surroundings and allows them to find places to hide and rest undisturbed.

In a house with several cats, the group leader usually occupies the highest perch, showing the importance of elevated space. You can find different cat perches in pet stores, but make sure they are safe and can support the weight of one or several cats.

If your cat likes to climb on high shelves, on top of the refrigerator, or in cabinets, make sure the area is free of objects that could hurt or trap. Also, beware of objects that the cat may accidentally knock over.

Providing cats with safe, elevated places to explore and rest is a great way to satisfy their instinct to climb and also provides them with an enriched and stimulating environment.

When they scratch

Another common behavior of cats is scratching, as it is part of their nature. Some cats may even kick the area near the food bowl or litter box, mimicking their instinct to bury and cover their tracks. Scratching is a natural activity for cats as it helps them keep their nails clean and also marks their territory. To prevent cats from damaging furniture or walls, it is advisable to provide them with more acceptable options, such as scratchers.

Cats often prefer to scratch on surfaces with attractive textures, so you can discourage them from scratching in unwanted places by placing double-sided tape or aluminum foil in those areas. In addition, you can teach them to scratch acceptable objects and redirect their scratching behavior to suitable places. With patience and consistency, you can reduce unwanted scratches at home and provide your cat with a satisfying alternative to express the natural scratching behavior.

Curiosity

They are very curious and prone to curling up in a tight ball to sleep, which gives them warmth and security. A similar behavior is to laze when they bend their legs to resemble a loaf of bread. This is done not only to look cute and take pictures but also to regulate body heat. Cats' behavior is the result of curiosity, although they may seem to try to write on the computer or enjoy pushing elbows, this way of being is common in many, only as a game mode. In addition, they may enjoy watching humans react to their antics.

Pay attention to how the cat plays and take note if this changes, if it does, it may be a reason to take it to the vet.

Temperament and behavior

Those who love cats want to develop a strong bond with these felines, but just like with people, some cats are more sociable than others. Some cats may be more independent and appear distant or bitter, while others are more open and affectionate.

Cats learn social behaviors primarily from their mother and littermates. This includes learning to control the bite and retract the claws during play. Play between kittens involves using teeth and claws, which can continue into adulthood. Kittens must have the opportunity to interact and learn social skills from other cats for healthy development.

Cats also learn by observing, imitating, and experimenting. It is essential not to separate kittens from their litter too early, as they need time to learn how to socialize properly. Being with their mother and siblings, they learn to understand and communicate with other cats and, in some cases, humans as well.

Another behavior that cats learn is hunting, both real and in the form of play. Domestic cats maintain their hunter instinct and may engage in behavior that combines hunting with play. In the home environment, cats can simulate hunting using toys, while outdoor cats can develop and hone their hunting skills.

Modify nighttime behavior

The story goes that bobcats are nighttime, resulting in domestic cats showing great energy in the middle of the night. It is not surprising that the cat wakes you up because it is running, knocks something down, and looks like it is going to end the decoration.

This can be fun at first, but it is a behavior you can modify soon by playing with the cat before going to bed. You can get another cat, but that can result in two crazy people knocking the house down.

With patience, you should gradually be able to modify the schedule so that the cat sleeps more at night.

Talking cats

Cats learn to meow so they can communicate with their mother. As they grow older, they learn to vocalize by howling, whistling, or growling to communicate with others. Many of them meow to communicate with humans, and of course, some talk more than others.

There are several reasons why the cat meows, such as hunger, loneliness, or just a way to say hello. Meowing can indicate injury or pain, so it always determines why it meows. Avoid punishing the cat for doing so, because in almost all cases, it communicates with you.

How to socialize your cat

Although many cats are affectionate, some need more time to be comfortable. There are shy cats by nature, while others have a history of trauma. Remember to be patient when introducing the new cat, and follow the tips to socialize correctly.

- Be patient and understanding.
- Start in small spaces so you can gradually become familiar.
- Keep things quiet and use a soft voice because they have sensitive hearing.
- Comfort with food.
- Let the cat approach and set the pace of socialization.

It is important that you do not get discouraged or give up, in addition, do not blame yourself or the cat, some cats need more work than others, and some are always shy and will avoid much interaction with humans.

Aggressive behavior

It is important to watch for signs of aggression in cats, as an aggressive cat can pose a danger in the home and cause painful scratches or bites that can lead to infections and illness. Cats may show aggression when they feel threatened or frightened. Some common behaviors that indicate aggression include a rigid upright posture with legs stretched out, stiff hind legs with the head lowered, direct gaze, whistling, or grunting.

Cat aggression can be related to pain or medical issues, so if the cat displays aggressive behaviors, it's important to take it to a pet care professional to rule out any health issues.

True, each cat has its personality and temperament, which can influence its level of sociability and desire for interaction with people. Some cats may prefer to be more lonely and not enjoy too much petting or being held, while others may be more affectionate and playful. It is important to recognize and respect each cat's differences and allow them to express their unique nature.

Cats make wonderful pets and can be amazing additions to the family. To foster a happy and healthy relationship with your cat, it's important to be patient, understanding and allow the cat to behave according to its nature. With patience and the right help, like the one provided here, you can create an environment where your cat feels safe and comfortable.

Coexistence

It's surprising to see cats and dogs being so different in many ways, but one thing they share is their positive reaction to a structure at home. Setting a schedule for feeding and playing with them is one of the steps I recommend to help reduce anxiety in cats.

Meeting your cat's basic needs in predictable ways can help to relax when you're not around. For example, if the cat knows that it will receive its food at a certain time, it is less likely to search for food constantly. In addition, implementing enrichment and exercise programs can prevent boredom and unwanted behaviors such as scratching furniture or running uncontrollably around the house.

Having a routine provides a sense of security to your cat, as they will know what to expect and when to expect it. In addition, a consistent routine makes it easier to live with your cat and can involve key aspects of training to teach some tricks and provide fun.

Routines benefit the cat and make your life more organized and simple. If you have children involved in cat care, a routine helps everyone remember to fulfill responsibilities, such as filling the cat's water bowl or administering medication if needed.

In short, establishing a routine for your cat is a great way to provide security, reduce anxiety and encourage a harmonious coexistence in the home.

Be a little flexible

It's contradictory to be told that flexibility is part of your cat's routine, but it is. Very structured schedules can leave your pet anxious when you're forced to stray from them. For example, if the cat knows that at 6 in the morning, you put the food on it, then

---

47

expects you to do it, but you did a project until 2 in the morning and want to sleep at least until 8, then the cat will start meowing at 6:15 because you have not attended to it.

You have to remember that the pet needs the structure and security of knowing that their needs are going to be met, but that there is flexibility for you to avoid anxiety in them from time to time.

What to include

Being a routine, think about the things that matter most, what you have in mind, it may be water, food, play, stimulation, and your sharing. These are important things to record yourself, but you also have to see the style of life and the needs that may vary. But here are some examples of how you can change the routine.

Example of a daily routine

- Start with a morning session of play and food. Play before you feed them, they are predators, and you go through the sequence of instinctive prey before feeding it is good. Follow this with the meal, and you will have started the cat's morning sequence of hunting, eating, grooming, and sleeping.

- Clean the litter box. Do this after feeding it, it is good, especially since you will surely have to go out.

- Break at noon. If you are lucky enough to be at home at this time, you can play with your cat for a while, both at that time and in the afternoon. If you're not home, leave some toys and mental enrichment to occupy the cat while you go out. Sleeping during the day will make them more awake at night.

- Game session at the end of the afternoon. This sequence of fresh prey for the cat at night is perfect before the meal is just what the cat needs. Use the toy wand to imitate birds, snakes, insects, and rodents. Let the cats look, jump, chase, and also bite for about half an hour. They can even play with the clicker.

- Dinner early. Many cats don't adhere to the strict schedule of two meals a day, so small, frequent feedings are the right thing to do. After all, in nature, they eat small meals like a bite during the day.

- Clean the litter box, you do it twice a day, it is one of the best ways to give a positive experience to the cat, do not forget to change the litter completely at least once a week.

- Then in the evening, one more sequence of prey with the cat followed by a delicious delicacy, this wears everyone down before going to bed and guarantees a restful night.

Stimulating the Senses

Provides exercise and enrichment to the house cat; This is good for helping the cat to be happy and healthy. After all, you'd be bored at home all day with nothing to do. Cats at home are not much different from wild cousins and maintain natural curiosity and many instincts, such as the need to hunt, climb or scratch. Having the ability to stimulate the cat and display its natural behaviors leads a cat to be well-adapted and entertained. Remember that a bored cat can create chaos, so offering space and opportunities for exercise will help avoid problems with them.

I leave you a series of things to do for you to stimulate at home.

Use the magic wands and teaser

Wands and teasers give the cat something to chase and harness hunting instincts.

- You can leave them aside to see it.

- When they see it, they will go out and catch that prey.

- In the end, save the toy so that there are no accidents when you are not with them.

To look for food

Here's how you can do it:

- Try to hide some food from the cat so that it hunts it.

- Start easy, you hide them where your cat can see them.

- Gradually, you increase the challenge so that it costs the cat more to find it.

- Having fixed times for meals and short spaces for feeding helps to imitate the eating habits of a wild cat and stimulates the natural behaviors of the indoor cat.

Leave puzzle toys

These toys are ideal for the cat to hunt food and help perform tasks and exercises. You can get a snuffle mat, a lick mat, or a puzzle mat.

Rotate your toys

In addition to the previous ones to play with, you can have many toys that have or do not have grass, mobile toys with batteries, or even ball pools. Remember to rotate them every so often so you don't get bored soon and don't look at them.

Leave hangers

Cats love to put themselves in high spaces that help them calm stress and see everything.

Have high spaces for them to exercise at home by climbing and jumping. The high vantage point also allows them to see more and window hangers are good for stimulating the house cat to see the outside world.

Put poles for them to scratch

Later I will discuss this in more detail, but I anticipate that scratching is a natural behavior that keeps the claws healthy. The poles give an outlet to the natural behavior, and you will prevent them from scratching things.

Place tall plants and grass for cats

Another normal behavior in them is chewing and the wild usually eat plants. You can combine the two by growing safe plants or a tub of grass for safe exploration and chewing. Remember to eliminate the toxic ones or leave them in spaces where the cat cannot access them, you can leave the chews, such as fish jerky, to nibble them.

Make a cat playground

If you have space to do so, you can make a play area that helps entertain the indoor cat with safe spaces overhead, give it a space to climb, and put a tree or wheel on it and teach it how to use it, this can be stimulating.

Let them watch TV

Play a video of birds, fish, or whatever interests them, so you can be stimulated and make it a great source of enrichment for your cat.

Allows secure access from the outside

Being able to explore or see the air in a safe and controlled way gives a lot of stimulation, you can give your cat a catio, a window hanger or a window box, you can put the cat in a harness on a leash and take the cat for a walk to explore the outside safely while exercising.

Set up odors

Something important to do is to stimulate their senses, it is often something that is overlooked, and catnip is the best to stimulate and entertain them because it has synthetic pheromones that help them with positive interactions, such as playing with others or pets, while also helping them calm down.

Play together

There are various games you can do with your cat, such as fishing indoors, this is enough to put floating toys in a bucket of water and let the cat try to catch the swimming prey.

You can also play fetch, which may require some training. Cats seem to enjoy it almost as much as dogs, which is a great entertainment exercise for the cat.

Teach them tricks

Contrary to what is believed, cats can be trained, as I told you before, so you train it, you stimulate it a lot and give it physical exercise, so you give it a valuable space with you, then you can try to apply what I taught you, then and follow it.

Spend time together

One of the best ways to give wealth to the indoor cat is that you spend time with them. They can play together, groom, or caress. Many cats just enjoy being in the same place as you, so they can sit together and hang out, you get a book, and the cats lie next to it, they are already happy.

Positive relationships between cats and owners make them feel more likely to play and keep them entertained.

Make a fortress

When you make the bed, fluff the sheets and blankets so they nod gently on the cat. You will end up enjoying this area as much as the cat.

Share non-toxic cooking herbs

Herbs such as dill, basil, and rosemary are safe for your cat to eat. If you can share, you can place them for you to cook.

Rearrange furniture

Furniture that is strategically placed allows the cat to jump progressively higher, imagine the athleticism it takes to move from the floor to the back of an armchair, to the shelf of a bookcase, and to the top of the rest front.

Rearrange the furniture, which is an excellent thing, so that you know how the cat and the changes in the environment. If they're excited and eager to explore or are more suspicious about the change in the environment, can help you customize the cat's enrichment to fit their personality.

Play hide and seek

Another great task you can do is to open magazines or newspapers on the floor and make a toy to throw cats go underneath and then come out again; that simulates small prey that enters and leaves the grass, and with this, the cat will be delighted.

Another variable of the hide-and-seek game is that you hide and wave a bag of goodies so that it follows the sound and finds you.

When you do, you reward it. While they are playing hide and seek, you can call them by their first name to locate you.

Boxes

Leave the shipping box of things bought online out of the cat's reach a few days before recycling it, cats are attracted to confined spaces where they can sleep. Leave the top open or close it, and cut a large space on the side of the box. Keep your camera handy because pictures of cats in boxes are great.

Take a break in nature

Looking for something from the outside, like a branch, a rock or fresh leaves, cats read the outside world when they smell new and earthy things.

Design a Scratcher course

You can make or build vertical or horizontal scrapers for the cat unless you know that it prefers one over the other. Make sure the vertical ones are at least three feet high and the horizontal ones one foot wide so they scratch comfortably.

You can have fun with Snuffle Mat

This is another enrichment tip for cats.

- Fold a towel. Tuck some treats inside between the folds.
- Put it inside a large paper box or bag for the cat to explore.
- Stimulate the animal instinct with a grass box with folds of goodies between the blades or put a snuffle mat inside the transported so that they have to hunt the food.

Go fishing

- Take a bowl, fill it with water, and add a rubber duck or wind-up toy.

- You put the bowl on a towel or floor tray and enjoy watching it splash. Make this an interactive activity by pushing the toy to keep it busy.

Clicker training

As I explained before, clicker training is wonderful because they bond a lot. Cats like it and are good at this. It will surely surprise you with everything it learns.

You can teach them things like a high-five, it's also a way for them to stimulate, they love to learn, and pieces of food are great treats. There are a lot of things they can learn. Create a repertoire of behaviors and show the brilliant ones to friends and family.

Chases the treats

If you give food to the cat, remove the bowl, put some excitement at the time of eating, and leave pieces for the cat to chase. If you leave it there to look for, they won't want to work for it.

Many cats love to chase treats, which is a fun way to keep them busy. If the goal is to burn energy, try throwing treats down the stairs.

Take a leash ride

Many domestic kittens love wild adventures, so encourage yours to do it, go for a walk. I advise you to train them to accept the leash and harness and choose a place where they can pass it, such as the garden.

Walking on a leash is one of the best ways to enrich the life of the cat, after learning to accept the harness, you can enjoy together.

Chapter 4: The Art of Communication (or the Lack of It)

Surely you feel that your cat sometimes talks to you, looks at you, and makes meows or movements where you want to know what your cat wants to convey to you. Sometimes you get to understand it, and other times you are not able to. In this chapter, I will show you each of the body language and verbal signs of your cat so that they can establish better communication.

Deciphering Body Language

There are a fair number of physical cues of a cat's mood, but their meaning may differ depending on the context. An example is that a confident cat has its tail raised vertically in the air. This tail position often indicates that the cat is comfortable and open to interaction. But on some occasions, such as protecting itself from a stranger in its territory, the high tail may indicate that the cat wants to attack. The high tail can represent confidence or potential aggressiveness, depending on the environment where it is. So, when it comes to reading body language, the key is that you are attentive not only to the physical but also to the context in which the cat is, which is the approach I want to show you in this chapter.

When considering context, it's good to try to see things from the cat's point of view. People who approach with good intentions may scratch or bite them and then blame the cat for being bitter. What's missing is an assessment of how the cat may have perceived the gesture. You should always consider whether the situation feels safe for the cat or might be frightening or anxious. A dark, confined environment that a cat can't easily leave creates more stress than a spacious, comfortable room where the cat can see the surroundings, so cats love to relax in open spaces.

The open or closed position of the body

It's good to remember that as animals, cats have evolved as prey and predators. When they find themselves in threatening situations, they feel preyed and frightened. When frightened, they may try to protect the body however they can and shrink into a small, unexposed position. A tense posture that looks like a ball may be a sign that they are in pain.

When the cat stretches, it voluntarily exposes itself, showing it does not feel threatened. But if the cat gets like a ball, it usually doesn't feel open to advances. A worried or anxious cat may bend down and stick to the ground. If they stop or freeze when they see you, they probably won't feel safe through your presence.

If you notice that the cat is put in closed positions, for example, when strangers come, but have no space to go to, consider putting high perches so that it is located there and is safer.

There is a big difference between a cat that stretches to relax and one that gets bigger as a way to defend itself. When they are afraid or angry to the point of being ready to fight, they can put their back up and stand on their side before the threat, this is terror, and they are ready for whatever comes.

If the back is arched and their hair stands up, this is called piloerection at the scientific level. These behaviors make the cat seem bigger and more intimidating. A cat displaying these behaviors may be ready to fight.

If the cat puts itself in a low back and tail position and stretches its front legs, it has just stopped and is taking a stretch to take three steps and lie down again.

It is good that you keep in mind that the body's orientation has its language, cats predict the intentions and movements pointing the body in the direction to which they will surely go. If the cat is on its side, it may feel shy and think about escaping. With a sideways position, it has the advantage of being able to take off quickly if there is a chase.

A crouching position allows the cat to jump and start running fast in case there is a need.

When the cat points its body and head at you, it may have interest and receptivity to advances. But, a cat that looks away may not necessarily be disinterested, the fact that it lets its guard down also indicates comfort and willingness to be touched. So look at the context.

A cat on its back, also known as "Venus' cat trap"

Again, no unique sign or indicator in body language is guaranteed, so you should be cautious when interacting with them.

Proof of this is that you can wonder if you have ever been a victim of the Venus cat trap, after you see the cat comfortable with the belly up, you touch it, and it convulses and clings with claws and teeth as if it expects you to touch it, this they do especially with those they do not know.

This trap can be avoided with a little care and sensitivity, the cat lies on its back, puts its belly, and shows relaxation, confidence, and security. In another context, the cat indicates that it is ready to fight because the position allows it to bite and seize.

The tail: a barometer of trust

The cat's tail is one of the first places to see when you want to know the mood. As I said before, a high and vertical tail is that it feels confident, happy and friendly, a low tail indicates that the cat is anxious or afraid.

It's good to think about how you make the cat feel comfortable and how it relates to situations in general. A cat with fear may not only have its tail down but present a smaller possible target for aggressors. A tall, swollen tail may indicate that it seeks to become larger for intimacy with enemies.

Why do they move their tails?

Another action that you can find in the cat is that they move the tail fast or slow. When the tail starts to shake, it may be that the cat is cheerful and excited. It may be similar to the vibratory moment you make before spraying something with urine. Again, context is all here, if the cat greets you and wags its tail, it's happy to see you.

On the other hand, it can be a sign of agitation and alertness, in a bad mood, and sometimes even a poisonous trap can show that it has no receptivity wagging its tail. When given attention and affection, the cat can go from excitement to just being tolerant and then getting upset. Body language gives clues and tells if you have to back off.

Wagging the tail does not always indicate agitation. Cats that engage in hunting behaviors, whether real or playing, wag their tails while they see prey. If you use a toy and the cat is crazy about it, your cat may be wagging its tail before jumping.

In this case, the movement of the tail indicates that it is stimulated and alert.

Ears: to hear and to show

The ear position is another space for you to see mood clues. Normal forward ears indicate that they feel confident, relaxed, or engaged. You should still see the context so that you understand better.

If a cat's ears stand, it is increasing the position as much as it can, and you may think it is comfortable, but sometimes the high and upright position of the ear is a sign of alertness or a desire to play. A cat with back ears is usually a good sign of anger or fear.

When the cats protect their ears and crush them to the side, it is almost certainly afraid. Some refer to ears as well as airplane ears.

Eyes: the windows of mood

The cat's tail, posture, and ears surely tell you what you need to know, but if you're still unsure, look at the eyes. When the cat trusts you and feels comfortable, it may blink slowly. The cat that blinks slowly is usually comfortable.

A cat's pupils are another way to tell how relaxed or stimulated it is. Relaxed eyes are usually part of a comfortable cat. When the pupils are large and dilated, it means that it is stimulated.

Stimulation is usually neither good nor bad; a playful cat may have dilated pupils, but it can also indicate fear, excitement, or anger. Consider this before deciding how to approach the cat.

The famous slow blink

Cats blink slowly to show affection and relaxation. If the cat does it slowly, it does not feel threatened by you, the cat trusts you. For you to bond with the cat, blinks slowly, it is a way to communicate.

Whiskers

If you assimilated the other signs of the cat and want to know more about how to read the language, in addition to posture, tail, ears and eyes, the whiskers will not tell you much, but they leave you more clues.

For example, cats with fear bring whiskers to their face, it is one more action of the tendency to try to become smaller. When they are confident, they can push the whiskers forward.

Actions it can do to tell you a message

Identify these communication behaviors, part of communicating with these cats is based on seeing how they behave around. Some behaviors have consistent meanings in a variety of cats.

- When it rubs with you, it is marking the property.

- The nose kiss is a feline affection that likes you and feels comfortable with you.

- If the cat rubs its head, flank and tail, the cat is showing a salute.

- Headbutts, as a game, are a sign of friendship and affection.

- Sniffing the face is to confirm identity based on the familiarity of the smell.

- If the cat rhythmically kneads its legs alternating between the right and left foot, it is a sign of happiness, satisfaction, or joy. Kneading is an indication that your cat knows and trusts you.

- When licking you is a sign of trust, you can be considered part of the family, like a mother who cleans cats.

- Your cat tries to eat your hair and may try to groom you, which means your cat loves and trusts you.

- Some cats show that they love you by copying what you do. You can try playing dead. They can sniff or nudge you, even play dead.

- If your cat bites you softly, it is a warning to leave it alone.

Vocalizations and Their Meanings

Although it is not body language, the noise that the cat makes is verbal language, they are the obvious way the cat expresses what it feels.

I start with purring, a good part of cats understand that purring is a good sign, moreover, like many other indicators, it is not guaranteed. Purring is a sign of pleasure, it is the most obvious way to see if it is happy, but as I said before, if it purrs in scenarios that it did not before, it can be a sign of illness or stress.

The fear/aggression vocalization series

When the cat wants you to understand that it feels a threat, it can go through vocalizations, increasing the intensity while increasing the discomfort. First, your cat starts growling. The growling cat warns you to back off, the next thing it does is a hiss, the reason it hisses is that they indicate that it feels a threat and may be prepared to fight or flee. It's also a way to show a potential aggressor that your cat has weapons with sharp fangs. The howl usually comes after the whistle. The squealing cat feels it has no options and is about to resist or retreat.

Squeaks and chatter

These are two vocalizations that are expressed for the same reason. The cat gurgles and chatters if there is potential prey in the window, may see an insect that wants to capture, but the cat is safe behind the screen, the chirps and chatters indicate tempered excitement because the cat is frustrated.

The threshing floor

Threshing is like a kind of purr but louder, almost like a bicycle bell. Cat moms chirp to communicate with kittens. When they do, they may feel friendly and familiar. Cats often chirp at owners to greet them.

The constant meow

Meowing is one of the most ambiguous types of vocalizations a cat has. When it meows, it does so for many different reasons. It can mean almost anything, from hunger to wanting to chat.

Like many other body language signs and behaviors cats display, meowing should be seen as part of the cat's larger context. However, constant meowing may indicate that something else is wrong. If they don't stop and feel pain, it's time to take them to the vet. If they meow daily, even after eating, they may simply be very talkative cats, as some cats and breeds are more vocal than others.

Cats have gained a reputation for being difficult to read, but it's not their fault, they simply communicate differently than humans. Observing their posture, tail, ears, eyes, whiskers, and verbal language is essential to understand if they feel comfortable or not.

The cat's body language and behaviors should be seen as part of the big picture. Using the context of the whole situation, trying to see things from the cat's point of view, and paying attention to the more subtle cues are ideal opportunities to understand your cat.

Bridging the Communication Gap

People always say that the key to successful relationships is knowing how to communicate, but for many, there is an important member who simply refuses to engage in dialogue. Whether they hide under the bed, push off counters, or purr in your lap. Cats are mysterious and fickle companions.

If your cat talks too much, to the point of being annoying, before you stop this, you must determine why the cat does it, analyze the circumstances around that meow, and take note of what seems to trigger it. When you've identified it, you can work on controlling vocalizations:

- If the cat meows to greet you, it is unlikely that you can do much to change it and come on, if it greets you that way, you have to be very upset to want to remove it from its habits.

- In case your cat meows to get attention, teach it that you will only pay attention to it when your cat is quiet. Resist the temptation to yell at the cat or pay attention, even if angry. On the contrary, be patient, wait a moment, and then provide the attention it wants. If your cat starts meowing again, you walk away and come back when the cat calms down. If you are constant, you will notice it.

- If you think your cat cries with loneliness because you spend a lot of time away from home, consider having a pet sitter come daily to feed the cat and play for a while.

- When your cat meows for food and stops feeding as soon as it cries, you give it food at the stipulated times so that the cat learns that it is useless to ask at other times. You can buy an automatic dispenser for you to schedule the times when it will release its food. It may meow at the feeder before it does at you. This is very useful if your cat wakes up in the morning and you want to sleep for another while, it will have its food and will not wake you up.

- If you have put the cat on a diet, consult with the doctor about the foods or supplements you can give it so that the cat feels satisfied with the food you put in.

- In case the cat is not prone to gaining weight, consider leaving food dry all the time so that it does not go hungry, if you give the cat diet food high in fiber, the cat can feel full without eating too much. Consult your doctor before doing so.

- When meowing to let the cat in or out, consider placing a cat door so you don't have to be the porter, I advise you to keep the cat inside to protect it from dangers and diseases. If this is one of those who usually goes out and you want to keep it inside, it may spend some time meowing, looking for a way out and being escapist. There is no way to overcome this, but as long as it does not come out, in the end, it will adapt to the interior and stop meowing so much.

- You can make an outdoor cat enclosure so the cat can spend time there, worse safely.

- If you have an unspayed cat who meows a lot from time to time, it may be jealous. Cats in heat are usually more loving and rub more, purr, roll on the floor, and meow a lot. This lasts about 4 to 10 days. The unspayed cat that is not bred, that has no relations with a male, will remain in heat every 18 to 24 days in the breeding season, which is about February to September for the Northern Hemisphere. Indoor cats can continue to go into heat all year round. The best way to reduce this is to sterilize it.

- If the male cat is not neutered and every so often meows too much, the cat may smell a cat in heat and want to go for a piece of cake. Then the cat will walk without rest, meowing a lot and asking to leave. Unless you can avoid this, the best way to reduce it is to castrate it.

- When an older cat starts meowing a lot, take the cat to the doctor to check for medical conditions, sensory deficits, and cognitive dysfunction. Medication will help.

Here's what not to do:

- Do not ignore the cat when it meows. The only exception is if you know that your cat meows for something that is not serious but seeks attention, and you want to cure that vice. In other cases, it is best to assume that something is wrong. The cat may not have access to the litter box, the water container may be empty, or it may be enclosed somewhere. Make sure the needs are met before you think it's just meowing out of annoyance.

- Don't scold or hit them for it, while punishments may make them run away, they may not have a lasting effect on their behavior. Not to mention that they will become fearful.

Cats love when you talk to them, although this is impossible to confirm at all, cats have strong ties with humans, and you do not dare to continue conversing with them.

Many people tend to talk to you as if they were babies, which has advantages, according to studies, the absence of harsh sounds when you speak is positive. Low-frequency noises like grunts are threatening, so it can be assumed that sticking to a higher pitch may be less threatening. Many cats fear loud noises, so they prefer that you speak to them more quietly.

Match the pitch to the command

Although cats are fluent in body language, they also understand the tone of your voice more than actual words. That you use a light and happy voice while telling them to get up from a place or to stop scratching a space will only confuse them and think that you are comfortable with what they do. But if you speak to them in an authoritarian way and a lower tone with a *"NO"* or *"LEAVE THAT,"* they will know that they do not have to continue as they go. In the same way, a higher and more cheerful tone when you praise them, call them, and give them something exciting, or a toy will let them know that everything is going well.

Match gestures and words

Combining tone with gestures and movements will help you convey the point of view. For example, you point at them on the floor or move downward with your hand while ordering them to get off a place. You wave them at you or call them with your index finger, indicating that you are calling them.

Beware of eye contact

Cats detect eye contact, they may stare at you to attend to it, and returning that look for a long time can be taken as a threat. You should know when the cat is shaking to look into your eyes, if the pupils dilate, they may indicate excitement or aggression.

Mimicking blows to the nose and head

Another way in which the cat shows affection is with blows to the head or nose, they may gently return the blows to the head and give you a purr of pleasure. This initiates a nose bump and extends a knuckle to their level, inviting them to sniff.

How to know if your cat is listening

Cats love when you talk to them, it may also depend on the message you give them, but it is not difficult to know if they hear you.

- If the cats headbutt back or rub their face, you know they're happy to see you.

- If they turn around and show you their butt, it is not that they disrespect you, but that they greet you friendly.

- When they respond to your affective proposals with a purr, you know they understand and return the love.

- When they envelop you with a slow blink, they entrust life to you.

- If they bite, scratch, growl, or wag their tail a lot, you know they don't like what you do or that you overstimulate them, and they want space.

- If they respond to the baby language you make and meow at you, it is an invitation for you to continue talking to them.

- When they turn around and expose the belly, it is not that you rub them, it can be a sign that they feel good or maybe you want to caress them. You will know the cat's body language that, although very similar, can have variations according to the personality.

You already know how to talk to cats, it's time to try what you've learned with yours, who will undoubtedly be surprised when your cat sees that you finally understood its love language.

Chapter 5: The Zen of Scratching

Cat scratching is key, they do it for various reasons. Okay, they're cats, the problem is when they do it on furniture and our stuff.

In this chapter, I want to show you how to provide suitable surfaces for the feline to scratch and learn to encourage healthy habits and tricks to put its claws where you want and not where it imposes.

In the end, I will leave you creative ideas to protect your things when you cannot deal with this stubborn who keeps insisting on burying sharp nails anywhere.

Providing Surfaces Suitable for Scratching

Before I give you the right scratching solutions, I should tell you why some things are attracted to them more than others. Cats and nails go together like peas to pods. What's more, cats need to scratch to be physically and mentally healthy. Cats scratch to stretch and exercise muscles, ligaments, and tendons and keep claws healthy. They do this because it helps them relax and vent if they're stressed. Scratching serves to mark the territory because they leave visible marks and smells that they feel for other cats to perceive. Cats scratch because they like it, it doesn't matter if they do it on a 3 thousand-dollar furniture. It is part of nature, they scratch trees because they are a precious substrate to scratch, as wild cats have always done. They are perfect for helping them achieve their goals.

- Strong and massive trees allow them to stretch and work their legs and shoulders without fear of injury.

- The bark of trees is crushed well under the cat's claws, and they are rough enough to retain odors under the scent glands of the paws, so they can give territory messages to other cats.

- Trees have many surfaces to scratch, so they can exercise various muscle groups and avoid getting bored. There are limbs, fallen branches, and various trunks that allow them to be scratched at different angles.

Posts that imitate trees

You can prepare the space for the cat at home, think about the trees, and generate strong and resistant poles with rough surfaces but crushable at various angles. They love sisal fabric for scratching, and corrugated cardboard is great but dirtier.

Make sure you have enough space to scratch if you have several cats so they don't fight for lack of space.

Have scratching surfaces in every area of the house. The cats will not want to look for a scraper when they want to use it, if they have one at hand, if not, they can choose a sofa frame, a chair, or a nearby frame. Good places to place the scraper are:

- Close to places where they usually spend time and where they sleep, they love to stretch and scratch when they wake up.

- Areas that have a lot of traffic in case. The cat will want to mark the area that many travel.

- On every level of the house. If your house has several levels, you will need a scraper in each one. There is little chance that a cat will suddenly feel the need to scratch on the third floor and go down to floor one to scratch, it will do so where it is born.

- Near windows. They love to see what's happening outside, so cat trees and condos are special when you put them near windows. If the cat sees an intruder outside, it can mark the territory and will have at hand, or the paw, the scratcher, to pull out the claws and mark.

- In hidden places, such as finding a scraper under the bed, you can buy additional inserts for angled scrapers and leave them in these places, so find and enjoy them.

Choose multiple scratch posts

After choosing where to place the posts for scratching and how much you need, ensure you have several of these. This will give the cat what trees do in nature, different angles and surfaces to scratch. Here are the types you might consider putting at home:

- The basic scraper, which is one of the safest to buy, meets the scratching needs of the cat, choose to be double thickness so that it does not fall and even be attractive to you.

- Basic post or hanger on it. Scratchers are great for cats if they also have how to lie on top. That's why a cat post with fabric above and a base can be put there and sleep a little high, and when the cat gets up, it's just stretching out and sharpening its claws.

- Cat tree: These trees give the cat vertical posts, either one or two, so they have a horizontal base where they can scratch at various angles, plus two heights where they climb and perch. Placing the tree near the window is an excellent idea to make them perfect.

- Condo for cats. If you have multiple cats, a cat condo is ideal. Several cats can use it and choose where they are going to scratch, either on the vertical or horizontal side and at different heights.

- Angled scraper. Small angled scrapers are perfect for providing some scratching environments for the cat. You can put them near the base of another scraper and tilt them in various ways in a more confined area. Cats love to have their feet on the ground and scratch upwards, then you turn up the angle and scratch at an upward incline.

Cats love various surfaces for scratching, so the more you place them, the better it will be for them to sharpen, and the less the claws will turn to your furniture.

Remember, cats like a variety of scratching surfaces, so the more you meet their needs with scratching posts, the less they will turn their claws to other items in your home.

Encouraging Healthy Scratching Habits

I told you before, scratching is part of the instinct of cats, they need to scratch. They do this to show emotions, such as excitement or stress, to mark objects with the smell. They have scent glands on their paws to remove the dead part of the nails and often just to be able to stretch.

It is also worth keeping in mind that cats do not think in terms of right or wrong, moreover, they have no concept of doing right or wrong. Cats think in terms of meeting needs. When the cat has the urge to scratch, the answer to where it should scratch is not what humans prefer or where it prefers to scratch.

As a cat owner, the goal is to give your cat the options they prefer for them and you.

Give your cat something to scratch that, from the point of view, is more desirable than the sofa or dining room legs

Cats prefer to scratch tall, sturdy objects that allow them to dig their nails and grip them well. That's why cats tend to scratch furniture. Many of these prefer the scraper pole when you buy it, which is at least 32 inches high so that it does not wobble when scratched and that it is made with sisal rope. Some prefer to scratch horizontally, in this chaos, place vertical scrapers on their side or find a resistant horizontal sisal scraper. Some cats love to scratch corrugated cardboard. There are ideal surfaces for scratching, like wood, so if you can ask your partner or even if you are a handyman, you can make the space for scratching. Just confirm that it is long and sturdy.

Put the scraper in a place where your cat wants to scratch

If you have the problem that your cat likes to scratch on the couch, put the pole next to the cat. In case the cat likes to scratch the wall, put it next to the front door. Location is key.

Introduce the cat in the scraper

You know you have the best surface for the cat to scratch, but that man does not know or is ignorant. The easiest way to introduce your cat to the pole is to play near it. For example, you can use the toy fishing rod or a laser light so that they interact with the pole in the middle of this site. They can rub catnip on the pole for the first few days. This usually causes the cat to investigate it. You mustn't take the cat to the scratching surface and rub its paws, this may look harmless, but it can generate stress in the cat, and can reject it.

Make objects it liked to scratch before become less desirable over time

For this part, you have prepared the cat to be successful when scratching the post or pad. If you have not yet realized how pleasant it is to do it in the scraper than in the furniture. It's best to dissuade the cat from objects you don't want them to scratch. For furniture, it is best to cover them with tight sheets. The blade will not be as desirable to scratch as the post with sisal. For smaller surfaces, you can use double-sided adhesive tape or any other element that makes the surface sticky, soft, or slippery. The cat does not like to try to dig its claws into any of these parts. Once your cat constantly uses the scratch post, you can remove the cover and leave your beautiful furniture again.

Don't cut their claws forever

This is known as declawing which is the amputation of the last bone of each toe. It's like cutting your fingers at the first phalanx. The method with which they do this is with a scalpel or with a guillotine, the wounds are closed with stitches or surgical glue, and the legs are bandaged. Laser surgery is also used, where a small, intense beam of light cuts through the tissue, heats, and vaporizes it. Both can cause lasting physical problems.

In many countries and New York, declawing has been prohibited. The Humane Society of America opposes declawing and tendonectomy, except in rare cases where it is necessary for medical purposes, such as removing cancerous tumors from the nail bed.

What is a tendonectomy?

This is when they cut the tendon that controls the nail of each toe. The cat keeps the claws but cannot control or extend them to scratch. It is a procedure associated with a high incidence of abnormally thick hoof growth. Frequent and challenging nail clippings are necessary to prevent cat nails from widening on people, carpets, curtains, and furniture or growing on the feline's paw pads.

Given the complications, the cat to which this intervention is done may need to have its claws removed later. Although it's not amputation, a 1998 study in the "Journal of the American Veterinary Medical Association" found that the incidence of bleeding, lameness, and infection was akin to tendonectomy and declawing.

Why is it bad to declaw?

This practice can cause paw pains, backaches, infections, tissue necrosis, death, and lameness. Removing the claws changes how the cat's paw touches the ground and can cause pain as if wearing uncomfortable shoes. Claws that remove incorrectly can grow back and cause nerve damage and bone spurs. For several days after surgery, a crushed newspaper is usually used in the litter box to prevent it from affecting amputated feet.

This unfamiliar substitute for the cat, accompanied by pain, can cause them to stop using the litter box; some cats can become bitten because they do not have claws to defend themselves. In my experience, I have encountered sad cases of this. I once saw a cat lunging against its sides in a cage because of the pain it felt after removing its claws. I swore at that moment that I would never have an animal like that or that I would do that to it, even if they scratched me anything.

Although sometimes, when I find an expensive curtain with a thread pulled and ruined, anger causes me to do it, I know it is the human side that manifests itself for a few seconds, but I would never do something like that.

Protecting Your Home

There are several ways in which you can protect furniture, I will tell you some:

Put a cover on the furniture

If what worries you most is what the furniture will have or that they are filled with hairs because of your cat, you can cover them with covers, purchase those that sell special for them, and put them on.

There are different types and fabrics. Choose the one you can easily clean or throw in the washing machine.

In case you do not want to have covers on the furniture because the plan is to show it off and not have them lined as if they were a wrapper, you can put towels where the cat rests, just remove this and wash it every day or every two days.

Spray a scent that scares the cat out of the place

Buy a repellent spray that the cat does not like and spray it on the areas where the gentleman is scratching it. You can buy deterrent sprays at almost all pet stores and follow the manufacturer's instructions.

You may have to throw more when the smell starts to go away. As additional advice, be careful with throwing the cat on top of it, don't be like that.

Water or compressed air sprayer

If you catch your cat scratching furniture, use water or a compressed air sprayer to create a negative association with that behavior. Do not spray the cat directly, but near it to avoid scaring it.

Cardboard or wood corner guard

I leave you some ideas for you to put together yourself.

Cardboard corner protector lined with fabric

To be able to do this, you will need:

- Cardboard (you can recycle old boxes).
- Fabrics (cotton, felt, or any resistant fabric).

- Scissors.
- Double-sided adhesive tape or adhesive tape.

Steps:

1. Cut strips of cardboard long enough to cover the corners of your furniture.

2. Line the strips with the fabric you chose. You can use glue or double-sided adhesive tape to secure the fabric to the cardboard.

3. Fold the lined strips in half to form right angles that fit the corners of your furniture.

4. Use double-sided adhesive tape to fix the corner guards in place. Make sure they are securely fastened so they don't slip.

Painted wood corner protector

To be able to do this, you will need:

- Wooden strips (they can be leftovers from previous projects)
- Acrylic paint or nail polish.
- Paintbrush.
- Saw.
- Sandpaper.
- Strong glue or small nails.

Steps:

1. Cut the wooden slats into strips about 10-15 cm in length.

2. Sand the edges of the strips to soften them and prevent splinters.

3. Paint the strips with colors that match the decoration of your home. You can use acrylic paint or even nail polish to give them a splash of color.

4. Once the paint is dry, join the strips together to form right angles that fit the corners of your furniture.

5. Use strong glue or small nails to attach the wooden strips and ensure that the corner guards are firmly attached to the furniture.

Cardboard corner protector decorated with wrapping paper

Here's what you'll need:

- Cardboard (such as cereal boxes or thick cardboard).

- Decorative wrapping paper.

- Scissors.

- Glue or double-sided tape.

Steps:

1. Cut cardboard strips that fit the corners of your furniture.

2. Line the strips with decorative wrapping paper. Use glue or double-sided tape to secure the paper to the cardboard.

3. Fold the lined strips in half to form right angles that fit the corners of your furniture.

4. Use double-sided adhesive tape to fix the corner guards in place. Make sure they are securely fastened so they don't slip.

Provides rest alternatives

If the cat has considered the couch as the throne on which to rest, then perhaps you should place other furniture where it lies. The cat tries to identify what attracts and then finds furniture for cats that it really likes best.

An example is if the cat likes high places and frequently climbs to the back of the couch, you get a cat tree with a base on top to sleep and even a toy. In pet stores, they sell many like this.

When you want to curl up between soft cushions, under the blanket, or on a closed bed, create something similar or buy it.

For the couch that is near the window and used to sleep while the sun caresses the cat, then put something similar that is in the window.

Optimizes litter box area

Cats can be very fussy about where they relieve themselves, and if they don't like the litter box, they may dirty the furniture as a sign that they tell you they don't like it. Make sure the litter box is quite large, as I explained then. This variety also serves to contain garbage and reduces the number of footprints on the floor and furniture.

Put a large mat under the litter box, this helps you catch the loose granules in the litter. Finally, consider using a heavier type of litter to further reduce tracking, but beware if the cat does not like it, it will not use it.

Pet your cat regularly

Use a stainless steel comb tool to remove the dead fur on the bottom. Brushing the cat every other day can greatly reduce the amount of hair on the couch.

A silicone brush for pets or gloves to remove hairs is great for collecting hairs that the cat and furniture have so you can remove them better.

CBD Oil

Scratching and dirtying a lot can also be a symptom that the cat has a lot of anxiety, especially when they show anxious behaviors such as frequent meowing, aggressiveness, hiding, attachment, and lack of appetite.

If you suspect that the cat is behaving with anxiety, CBD oil can help. Putting that on is easy, use a dosing dropper when the cat is calm. If it is scary, you can wrap it in a towel so you relax it and put the oil.

Keep in mind that although CBD is available in many places, there are somewhere they prohibit it, check the laws so that you do not commit any crime when trying to acquire it.

Vinyl nail caps

As I made clear before, removing the claws of cats is not an option because, in addition to removing them, you leave them almost crippled. The result will be various health problems and a lot of pain. I'm sure you don't want that. Not to mention the hostility, not using the litter, surely the remedy will be worse than the disease, and you will ruin your cat's life.

The medical or rather, bloody procedure is banned in dozens of countries. Instead, you better put soft covers that you stick on the cat's nail, it will continue to scratch, but the covers will prevent them from damaging anything. These fall off on their own within weeks when the cat's nails grow.

However, the only disadvantage is that not everyone gets used to the covers, and putting them on can be challenging if they do not like touching their legs. Your vet can help, although you should use this as a final resource.

Trim the cat's nails

It is one of the most obvious that you can take into account, keep the cat's nails well cut, although not so much, so that they are dull and do not generate damage. If the cat resists being cut, try wrapping it in a towel while you cut them, or take the cat to a professional who does.

Another way to encourage the cats to scratch where they should

Rub some catnip on the scrapers so that they get closer to them, you may have to put catnip to make them more interested. Even install several poles to scratch, especially if you love to scratch wherever you want.

Give them an award for good behavior

When you notice that the cat uses the scraper where it should, you can reinforce good behavior, and praise it with love or a treat. When you see that the cat scratches the pole, you say something with love, praising that the cat does it there, rub it behind the ears, and give it a treat.

Say NO and be consistent in training

When you see that the cat scratches the furniture instead of where it belongs, make a loud noise like applause and scare it, remove it from the furniture, and firmly say *"NO,"* do this every time you see it scratching where it should not.

Don't yell or get angry. Remember that it is a natural part of them that they want to scratch. This is to keep the nails trimmed. It is also a way to communicate with other cats.

Give them a scare when they do what they shouldn't

Some cats can keep scratching furniture even if you tell them no and push it away. Try to scare them whenever you see them acting badly. For example, if you see them jumping on the couch where you don't want them, walk to where they are and shake a can with a few pennies inside.

Keep in mind that normally this will only prevent the cat from scratching when you are around, you should combine this with other deterrents for bad behavior and rewards when it behaves well.

Make the cat active

Get the cat to stay active, they may scratch the furniture if they feel bored or need more attention. Spend time playing with it, and reduce bad behavior when it is activated and entertained. For example, you hang ribbons on a stick, throw balls or toys, or hide treats in puzzle balls for them to find.

Another tip that you can keep in mind is that you place elements to scratch, for example, buy a game tree that has a scraper. You put it near your favorite furniture or the window so they can see outside.

Chapter 6: When the Fur Flies: Dealing with Behavioral Challenges

Cats are beautiful, photogenic models by nature to fill thousands of pages with their faces, paws, and any position they adopt, but in addition to everything I have shown you in the pages, there are more challenges to face, and that is when they have certain behaviors that alter the harmony at home.

I explain several of their performances and how you can deal with them.

Handling of Territorial Aggression

Unfortunately, territorial aggression can be dangerous for you, other pets, your cat, and nearby animals. If the cat has become more and more protective and you wonder how to deal with territorial aggression in them. I'll tell you how to fix it.

All animals have the instinct to protect what is theirs, but some situations are worse than others, you must quell territorial aggression before they hurt anyone or something.

Where does territoriality come from?

It is difficult to blame a cat for being territorial and wanting to protect what it takes as its property. Cats are cats when they perceive someone or something as a threat. The resulting aggression can be directed at you, other humans, cats, dogs, and other animals. Cats tend to be territorial when it comes to their home, litter boxes, food, water, toys, and even owners. Although territorial aggression is normal, it must be controlled.

Signs that your cat is aggressive and territorial

In almost all cases, they do not go from 0 to 60 in an instant and give warning signs that they are territorial.

On a physical level, you can see body language and notice that it has signs that it is increasingly agitated or aggressive.

- The pupils dilate.
- The ears they put back.
- Turn their ears forward and then back.
- Lie down in a crouching position and stare at something or someone.

When it comes to behavior, it may have physical signs that can be a little difficult to detect if you don't pay close attention to it. Fortunately, cats also do some actions and have signs of behaviors that begin to feel territorial and aggressive. I leave you some of these to keep in mind:

- Begin to urinate on objects with territorial aggression. Marking the territory.

- Crouch down or stalk things and people they take as threats.

- Hiss or hit animals or people.

- Bite, scratch, or growl.

- Rub the body against objects to leave a mark on them.

As I said before, cats do not climb directly to attack, but they warn. But if they get very excited about something or are surprised, they may become territorially aggressive faster than they would otherwise.

Knowing how to deal with territorial aggression

Given how dangerous territorial aggression in a cat can be for you and others at home, it's good to train cat behavior. Territorial aggression can cause injuries to other animals, full blown fighting, and damage to furniture and objects.

Distract them

One of the ways you can avoid aggression is to distract them. When you notice signs of aggression, distract the cat with noises, sweets, or movements. They have a short attention span, which means they'll forget about the aggression if you distract them soon.

Separate them from the source of their aggression

If the distraction does not work, the best way to stop it is to move it away from the source, move the cat to a separate place, and close the door so that you have time to calm the cat down. Cats are solitary animals, which means that space alone gives you time to calm down. But be sure to take it to a place with treats instead of picking it up and moving it.

Reduces stimulation

Overstimulation can sometimes trigger your cat to engage in territorial aggression. If you notice your cat getting aggressive while looking out the window, close the blinds and don't let it see. It's similar to taking your cat to a room where it's going to calm down.

Don't try to pick it up

Something important to keep in mind when trying to prevent this aggression is that you should not pick it up. If it already has signs of aggression toward someone, it may redirect the aggression to you if you try to pick it up.

How to prevent aggression with your cat

Since your cat is difficult to stop when it gets aggressive, it's best to prevent aggression before it starts.

Socialize with the cat

Just as people get socially uncomfortable when they do not go out enough, the cats will not know how to act with others, and if they do not practice, they will get worse, so have a space for the cat and organize appointments to play with other cat owners, so they can share more and be less aggressive.

Sterilize or neuter

Have your cat spayed or neutered from a young age to prevent this territorial aggression. Territorial aggression is almost always related to hormones, which you fix with medical intervention.

Problems with the Litter Box

Before I show some problems and tips for the litter, I will leave you others and tips to treat them.

Aversion to Cat Litter

This aversion is described as the cat's way of avoiding using the litter tray, causing it to misbehave by leaving its feces anywhere. There are many reasons why they can reject the box, even if you have used it without a problem before. The fact is that it may be due to behavior, for example, the cat does not like the kind of litter you put on it, or it can be psychological, such as the cat was scared while in the litter and now associates it with fear. When they relieve themselves, cats are vulnerable and more sensitive than normal.

Cats often change their toileting behavior if they have problems with the litter tray. Once they start avoiding it, they may develop alternative preferences, such as urinating on particular surfaces, furniture, bed, bathroom or wherever, which can worsen things. If you think the cat doesn't like the litter you put on it or if you changed it recently, this may explain why it doesn't want to use it.

The choice of material is important and is personal for each cat. Some prefer agglomerating litter, and others non-agglomerating litter. Some want thin substrates, and others a little thicker. I advise you that many cats prefer binder, odorless, fine-textured litter, and natural substrates such as soil or litter. Many cats don't like plastic trays. It is good that you choose a suitable location, preferably a quiet and private place away from the feeding area, that is not unpleasant or unattractive to the cat.

Covered versus uncovered

Many cats prefer uncovered trays, while the lid gives privacy and a sense of security, it can also make them worry and feel confined. One that is covered can trap odors and unpleasant chemicals.

The advantage you have is that you will not smell what the king leaves there, but for the cat, it will be a problem, better to remove the cover if it has problems of use.

Inappropriate disposal

I leave you tips on how to treat the disposal of waste.

Don't throw it away

Some biodegradable hygienic litters claim to be disposable, but it's not the best thing to throw away that used litter. The cat's litter has gone through a process from agglomeration to perfumed. Unfortunately, disposing of it in the trash can clog septic tanks and sewer systems. Both garbage and feces contain harmful pathogens and toxins. This means throwing it in the trash can be just as bad as throwing the feces away.

One example is the toxoplasma parasite, which is harmful to marine life and people with weak immune systems. In addition, other parasites can cause diarrhea and be dangerous. Many municipal waste treatment plants cannot properly filter these pathogens, although I recommend contacting your local facility to confirm this. As a tip, don't dump waste into the sewer to avoid putting the community, wildlife, and waterways at risk with this waste.

Don't compost it

Technically you can compost cat poop if you buy some hygienic litter, but some recommend that you do not.

First, cat fecal matter contains parasites and other harmful organisms, such as toxoplasma, that can infect you and others, which is a health risk.

The other thing is that people should not try to compost with pet waste because they do not reach high enough temperatures to kill pathogens. The compost pile must reach 131 degrees Fahrenheit for the parasite to be killed, but compost piles rarely reach that temperature.

Don't bury the cat

Burying cat waste is also a problem for many reasons similar to those already mentioned. If poop doesn't biodegrade well in the compost pile, there's little chance it will do so underground. Waste organisms can leach into gardens or waterways.

Don't burn it

When you live in rural areas, you may think that burning poop with litter is an option, but it is not recommended. If you use types of litter, such as those containing clay, the waste will not burn completely. In addition, burning garbage, in general, is detrimental to both human health and global warming, as it can release harmful toxins and greenhouse gases that contribute to climate change.

So how do you get rid of poop? The best option is to place the lumps of waste in a double bag and put them in the trash can outside your home. It is advisable to use biodegradable poop bags to reduce the environmental impact, as they will increase the chances of the waste decomposing properly. However, not all bags claiming to be biodegradable have been properly tested to prove this, so it's important to research before purchasing.

Simply looking at the bag or reading the claims on its label is not enough. You should look for information about the tests and the conditions in which they were performed to support their claim to be biodegradable. If companies do not provide this information, it is advisable to be cautious and look for more reliable alternatives.

Beyond the bag you use, throw away the poop.

Ways to keep the box clean and free of bad odors

A stinky litter box does not amuse you and less the cat. The smell of the box can be a sign of the pet's health problems or your hygiene.

It's time for you to take action on this. The litter box has to have the same consideration as the other bathrooms in your house, it is more, I think the box deserves more attention.

Remember, the cat's sense of smell is 14 times stronger than yours, so if things smell bad, you will feel that smell and the cat much more, just as when they smell good or do not smell.

About 10% of cats suddenly refuse to continue using the litter box, and the smells in these are one of the reasons why they abandon it.

I leave you a series of tips to prevent the litter box from reeking like an interstate highway bathroom.

Choose the right brand of Cat Litter

Have you stood in the pet aisle of the store and seen the litter options available?

Wheat, corn, clay, grass, paper, so many options that you do not know which one to choose for your cat. To determine the best litter option you like, I leave you this tip:

- Buy small bags of different types of litter. Take out one cup of each type in a different container.

- Place a quarter cup of ammonia, although keep this away from the cat.

- Let the mixture sit undisturbed for several hours.

- When you're ready, smell each container of ammonia-soaked litter.

The nose will tell you which is the best for you to control odors. Keep in mind that cats do better when you place a litter little by little. You can mix the new brand with the old one for a few days until it gets used to the unfamiliar smell.

Sprinkle baking soda in your litter box

Baking soda is an excellent natural deodorant for cat litter boxes and is safe for them. Baking soda is completely non-toxic and can help absorb odors from urine effectively. It is a much safer and preferable option than scented options, as cats often detest artificial odors.

However, it is important to note that although baking soda can help control odors, it does not replace a constant and proper cleaning of the litter box. Collecting debris, refreshing and washing litter regularly is still essential to keep it clean and enjoyable for your cat. Baking soda is a useful supplement to reduce odors, but it should not be the only measure taken to maintain proper hygiene in the litter box.

Use carbon filters to minimize litter box odors

Eco-friendly carbon filters help you eliminate odors that remain. As with baking soda, charcoal is an affordable, all-natural, non-toxic control system.

Scented accessories

Many scented air fresheners smell great to you but gag cats. Worse, some products smell good but can harm your cat. Potpourri oil is an example, it can burn the cat's skin.

The all-natural cat odor filter is perhaps the best option, but if you like the house to smell pungent, try some non-toxic air fresheners.

Practice good hygiene in the litter box

The litter box cleaning schedule would have to be like this.

- Daily, take out the cat box, the clumping litter helps you with this.

- Refresh the litter completely each week, throw away the old, and add about 4 inches again.

- Every week, wash the box with warm water and a mild dishwashing detergent with no perfume.

- Every quarter it recharges and replaces the cat odor filter.

If around the box there are odors that remain over time, you can place some antibacterial solution that is safe for the cat. That you have clean the litter box can be an important step so that the feline litter smells good.

Put the box in a well-ventilated area

Some people hide the box in dark and secluded places such as the basement or garage, which is bad. Shy cats normally hate going to damp, dark, or lonely spaces to do their thing.

A harassing cat may take advantage of the isolation to start fights or prevent another small cat from using the litter box.

If you put the box where you can't smell it, you may forget to clean it regularly. Keep boxes in a socially appropriate place, such as the living room or guest bedroom. If you're going to be outdoors, choose an elegant box, so it won't attract the attention of nosy guests.

Talk to your veterinarian about your cat's diet

Spicy poop can be a sign of trouble. Ask your veterinarian or feline nutritionist to recommend a healthy and safe diet change. New foods can be a great solution to control the odors that you've been looking for.

That you have the home and the box clean and fresh is good for the cat's health and tranquility. Keeping the area box odor-free can make it easy for the cat to do things where it should, helping it be healthy and happy.

Controlling Bite Game and Aggressive Play

Cats need play, it is a vital part of their lives for their mental and physical health. It is especially important for indoor cats. Although they can sleep up to 16 hours a day when they are awake, they need stimulation, and the best way to achieve this is through play. In the wild, lions, tigers, and other wild cats spend their time hunting or teaching their young to hunt. Play with domestic cats is simply a way to channel that hunter instinct.

Hunting behavior in kittens begins early, as soon as they can stand on their paws. They stalk and pounce on their littermates. For this reason, it is always recommended to adopt kittens in the company of another kitten or a young adult cat. Playing with other cats not only provides them with companionship but also teaches them to moderate their rough behavior, as they learn that biting and scratching hurts.

Signs that it is biting

One of the most common signs of aggression in gambling is touching the ankle, which may be that you are walking and the cat suddenly grabs your ankle and scratches or bites you. Aggression in play can get your hands, especially if you use it to play with the cat, which can be cute when the cat is small but not so much when it becomes an adult.

There is a difference between rough play and aggression

Sometimes it can be difficult to tell the difference between rough play and aggression. It's a very fine line between these two. The cat sees the cat's body language looking for clues, the behavior may have jumps or lateral jumps, sometimes with the back arched.

During a fun game, the ears will be in the air, and there may be whistles, but the game is usually silent, if you notice that the cat's ears are put to the back of the head or hear the growls, the game turns into fighting.

Here are actions you can take to correct and prevent aggression:

Provides a variety of toys for your cat

The toys stimulate the cat's natural hunting instinct, which will more effectively create a fun play experience for the cat that further helps burn excess energy. Even though many cute toys are filled with catnip on the market, just putting one in front of the cat and waiting for it to play with it doesn't work for everyone.

Structured playtime

Play with the cat in regular spaces every day, at least twice a day for about 15 minutes, as I explained before. These play sessions will keep you happy and are a great way to strengthen your bond with the cat.

Set aside time for a couple of play sessions of about 20 minutes long, each day, you and the cat will find a space for these play sessions.

Get creative with playtime

Interactive toys like the fishing rod are the best way to make the cat play with you and satisfy its prey-hunting instinct. How you move the interactive toy is important. Do not shake it too hard, just give the cat aerobic exercise. This is how cats hunt naturally. You should stick to what is natural for the cat: in nature, the cat stalks its prey while remaining silent and invisible, gradually approaching until it is within striking distance and then jumping.

Cats don't have the lung capacity to chase until exhaustion, so don't do marathons all over the house. Move the toy as if it were prey, alternating between fast and slow movements so the cat has time to plan its next move. Another tip is that movements that move away from or cross the cat's visual field awaken its prey instinct. Don't hang the toy on the face or move it toward the cat.

If you use interactive puzzle toys, you can keep the cat entertained and mentally stimulated when they can't play together. These toys are designed to fill them with treats and challenge the cat to retrieve them through the openings they have. Turn toys in and out, don't leave the same toys in the same place every time. Save some and rotate their use weekly to prevent the cat from getting bored.

You do not need to buy expensive toys for the cat. Almost anything can be a toy: supermarket bags with cut handles, rolls of toilet paper, milk carton lids, and tissue paper, among others. In the cat's mind, everything is made to play. Some cats enjoy chasing bubbles or throwing swabs in the bathtub. Think like the cat, and you will be surprised to see all the options you have to play without spending money.

How to Redirect Aggressive Gambling Behavior

Keep these tips in mind:

Never play with your cats with your hands

Before I recommended it, but if the cat has this tendency, do not do it anymore. Cats may associate the hand with one more toy and won't understand why it's okay to grab and kick the mouse but not your fingers.

Distract the cat with the right toy

If you have an ankle gripper, have a toy with you, when you see that it is approaching, throw the toy in front of you to distract it.

Give the cat a break

For any play and interaction with the cat when they start to play rough, scratch, or bite. Leave the room or take your attention elsewhere. Do not lift the cat to remove it from the site, the energy will be increased to play and interact physically, which can lead to it becoming aggressive. Be consistent with this, don't inadvertently reward bad behavior.

Don't punish the cat

You should never yell at the cat, hit or chase it, and do not use spray bottles to correct its failures or what you do not like. Punishment only makes the cat afraid of you and becomes more aggressive. Besides that, you will ruin the bond with the cat.

Conclusion

If you got here, I want to congratulate you, it means that you love your feline and that you want the coexistence to be the best possible.

Surely this has been a journey of smiles, learning, and training for that furry that you love so much, but sometimes it generates one or another headache. You already understand the instincts, how the cat communicates effectively, and the positive reinforcement you gave with the training and corrections.

You embarked on this training which is a constant process knowing already that each cat is unique.

Embrace the joys you have with your cat, you know that they are enigmatic creatures in some things and predictable in others and that they are love, cuddles, purrs, and a little chaos because you have to be flexible, you will get a harmonious coexistence.

Felines have unique and subtle communication through their body language and vocalizations. I hope you already understand their behavior and need to provide them with a suitable and satisfactory environment.

The cat's body language, such as tail position, ears, eyes, and general posture, offers valuable clues about its mood and comfort level in various situations. Always consider the context in which the cat is since the same signal can have different meanings depending on the environment.

Scratching, although sometimes it irritates you a lot for what it does, is a natural and healthy behavior that allows them to keep their claws in good condition and leave a mark on their territory.

If you give your cat adequate options of scrapers and you take care of the nails, surely they will not scratch your furniture anymore.

Proper hygiene of the litter box is essential to avoid behavioral problems such as those I showed you at the time, imagine that by being irresponsible in cleaning, the king plants a gift on the furniture, worse than a scratch.

Don't forget that play is essential for cats' mental and physical health, especially those who live indoors. You can channel their hunting instinct through the game and keep them stimulated and entertained. Interactive toys and puzzles can be valuable tools to keep them happy and moving around the house without ruining everything.

It is good that you consider the environmental impact of your actions when disposing of litter and waste. Opting for biodegradable solutions and properly managing waste will help protect the environment and everyone's health.

Cats need encouragement to stay happy and healthy. Returning to scrapers, place vertical and horizontal ones, interactive toys, and structures for them to climb and hide. This will help you explore your surroundings and release your hunting instinct.

It generates regularity in their daily activities, such as meal and play times. Leave a consistent schedule that helps them feel more secure and confident in their environment.

Cats need places where they can retreat and rest undisturbed. Have soft beds and comfortable shelters in different areas of the house so they can relax. As for games, creating treat-hunting games, such as hiding treats in interactive toys or hide-and-seek, are great for keeping your mind active and encouraging your curiosity.

Some cats are more independent and may need moments of solitude. Learn to read their signs and respect when they prefer to be calm. Although if you have several cats, make sure they get along and offer opportunities for them to play and socialize. Proper socialization from an early age is also important for their emotional development.

Do not forget to provide them with periodic veterinary checkups, they are essential to keep them healthy and prevent health problems. Also, make sure you follow a proper vaccination and deworming program.

Sometimes they do things that make them lose the boxes but don't hit them, they don't respond well to violence or physical punishment. Instead, use positive reinforcement like rewards and praise to reinforce a desired behavior. Spend quality time with your cat, play with them, pet them, and observe them. You will learn to understand their needs better and strengthen your bond.

Cats are unique beings with individual personalities. Respect their nature and accept that they may be more independent or shy than other animals. Patience and unconditional love are key to a happy and harmonious relationship with your feline.

Understand and attend to the needs of your or your cats, so you can establish a closer and more satisfactory relationship with them, giving them the love, care, and respect they deserve as unique and special living beings.

THE AUTHOR

Ted Burton, besides being a champion of grilling and BBQ *(look at his book on Amazon: "Become a Grill Master")*, is an expert in domestic animals and their psychology: cats, dogs, and horses have been his passion since childhood. This passion led him to become a breeder, trainer, and veterinary assistant. Ted lives happily with 16 cats, 8 dogs, and 4 horses. With them, his family consists of 33 living beings.

Made in the USA
Las Vegas, NV
13 December 2023

82414760R00059